MYSTERY

on the

COURTHOUSE LAWN

REBECCA JANE CLINTON

authorHOUSE®

AuthorHouse™
1663 Liberty Drive
Bloomington, IN 47403
www.authorhouse.com
Phone: 1-800-839-8640

Published by AuthorHouse   03/07/2012

ISBN: 978-1-4685-6053-4 (sc)
ISBN: 978-1-4685-6052-7 (hc)
ISBN: 978-1-4685-6051-0 (e)

Library of Congress Control Number: 2012904388

This book is a combination historical fact and fiction. Some of the names have been changed, but all historical references, with a little fiction added, have been taken from many printed records (Newspaper Articles, the Ingham County Pioneer, written by D.B. Harrington, which he wrote in 1911), Mason's 125 Anniversary Book, etc. that tell the story of the founding of Ingham County and the City of Mason.

This book is dedicated to anyone who loves history, and is interested in learning some historical information about the City of Mason. I have always loved reading about everything, and hopefully you will enjoy learning about Mason and its' past.

CHAPTER 1

"OWWWW," I gasped. I guess I was staring out the window, because the next thing I knew Sister Helen smacked my hand with the ruler and told me to pay attention.

Sally, the girl that sat next to me, whispered "Betsy, I tried to get your attention."

"Thanks for trying to get my attention," I said. Boy, did I turn red when the rest of the class laughed.

Sister Helen said, "Ok, everybody be quiet."

My name is Betsy Slayton, and I'm 9 ½ years old. My mom, dad, brothers and sisters, and our dog Taffy live in the big house on South Jefferson Street next to the old Stand Pipe.

It's late spring in 1960, and I'm finishing my fifth grade year at St. James Catholic School on West Elm Street. It's only a week till school ends for the summer, and I can't to see what 6th grade will be like in the public Junior High School in the fall. The Junior High School is down on the next block from our house.

Not that I don't like Catholic School, but these nuns can be pretty strict, and if you do the least little thing wrong, there is always, "The Ruler."

From where I sit in the classroom, I can look out the window and look down the street and see the railroad tracks and the bridge. From there, it goes directly uphill.

On one side of the street, are the stairs that go to the Junior High School, and on the other side are the Indian Trails that run along the railroad tracks in back of the houses. We call them the "Indian trails", because of all the arrowheads we have found when playing. It's very steep and climbing them can be a pain.

It seemed like it took all day for 3:00 to come. I got out of there as fast as I could, because my younger brother Todd found out what happened and wore that funny smirk on his face, which meant I'd better get home before him.

CHAPTER 2

Guess what! He beat me home and was in the process of telling mom about what happened to me at school. When I walked into the kitchen, mom was shaking her head. I gave Todd the evil eye and was going to push him out of the kitchen.

Mother said, "Betsy, stop picking on your brother."

Todd is my younger brother by 14 months. He is always trying to get me into trouble, but we are close, and most of the time do everything together.

Mom stated, "What were you doing that made Sister Helen hit you with the ruler?"

I looked at mom and said, "I guess I was staring out the window, looking at the hill in back of the house."

"Go up to your room and do your homework before dinner," Mom responded.

Dad got home from the office just about dinner time and said, "Hi Honey." By that time Mom had forgotten all about it. After dinner I asked her and dad if I could watch a little TV before I went to bed.

Gunsmoke was on at 8:00 PM, and it was one of my two favorite westerns. I've always like the old west, and when I could would wear my cowboy boots, my pistol, and my cowboy hat. I liked the old west, and ever so often some of the episodes bothered me when it got to killing and hanging. I liked Marshall Dillion, Miss Kitty and Festus.

The episode was called "Hot Spell", and Matt had to protect a gunman, Cope Borden, from being lynched. The weird thing was that the normally law-abiding citizens and ranchers and cowhands were the ones who wanted to see Cope Borden lynched.

I didn't really like this episode. It made me feel sad to think that law-abiding citizens could do such a thing. But it was a different era than what we lived in.

Before Gunsmoke ended, Mom came into the den and said, "Betsy it's time to go to bed."

I went upstairs to bed and Mom came up to tuck me in and gave me a kiss goodnight.

The rest of the week went by without incident, and before I knew it I had graduated from the fifth grade. I went around to all the sisters, even Sister Helen, and said my goodbyes and told them how much I'd miss St. James.

I walked up the hill to the house and looked back at St. James with tears in my eyes.

I couldn't wait to start my summer vacation, but little did I know that the next few weeks would be the strangest my brother, my cousins and I, would ever experience.

CHAPTER 3

When I got home, Mrs. Adams was in the dining room ironing clothes. "Hi, Mrs. Adams," I said. Mrs. Adams was a neat older lady, and I always had a good time talking with her. She would always tell me stories about what was happening on the farm.

We all ate dinner later, and since it was a Friday night, I asked mom if I could stay up later to watch Bonanza. "I guess so, but then it's time for bed," Mom said.

Bonanza came on and it was the episode I always laughed at. It was about little people that came to the Ponderosa to pan for gold so their families could make a home for themselves.

They got away from their circus manager and were hiding on the Ponderosa when Hoss saw them. Hoss got the funniest look on his face, when he saw the little people.

Then the next thing you know their manager comes to town looking for them, and Hoss goes to the saloon, and talks about the little people. Everyone in the Saloon goes to the Ponderosa to look for them. I laughed all the way through the show.

It was 9:00 PM, and I was getting tired and went up to bed. That night I had the weirdest dream.

In the dream I was up town at the County Courthouse watching some men plant flowers. As I was watching them dig the holes for the flowers, a small object came up with the dirt and flew a few feet away. The men didn't see the object and kept on planting the rest of the flowers, and it started getting dark. That's when I woke up.

The next morning I got up, forgot all about the dream and ate breakfast. My brother and I went out to the back yard and played horse on the fence. We'd put an old rug on top of the fence and get on and ride it. We got bored after a while and went back inside the house to see what mischief we could get into.

Todd and I always like to see how long it would take Mom to notice we were hanging from the railing on the stairs. We would try to be like Tarzan and swing.

If we fell, it wasn't that high. When Mom would come out of the kitchen, she would see our legs hanging and get upset. By that time we dropped to the floor, and smiled at her and she told us both to go outside and play.

The phone rang, and it was my cousin Mandy. Mandy and her brother Chase live two blocks away on East Cherry Street. Mandy asked, "What are you doing?"

"Not much," I replied. She told me that she and Chase, were going to walk up town, and did we want to go with them.

Mandy is my age, and her younger brother Chase is my brother Todd's age. I asked mom if it was ok, and she it was.

About 10 minutes later Mandy and Chase were at the door. After saying hi to mom, we all left the house and started uptown.

CHAPTER 4

We didn't have any plans at the time, and had already spent over half of our allowance for the week. We thought we would ask some of the store owners if we could do something in exchange for pop and candy.

As we walked past the Junior High School, I asked Mandy if she was going to be in the same class as I was. "I've got Mrs. Mills," Mandy stated.

"I got Mrs. Elliott and she and Mrs. Mills have their rooms right next to each other on the second floor," Betsy responded.

"Hey, that will be neat because we'll still get to talk with each other during our breaks," Mandy said.

As we walked past the Junior High, I asked Mandy if she wanted to see if there were any windows open, and see if we could sneak into the building. Mandy said, "Maybe we can see how long it takes the janitor to find us."

We all walked around to the north side of the building around by the tennis courts. There was always a window open a crack. No one was playing tennis on the courts, so we looked at the lower windows and saw one open a crack.

Since no one volunteered, I went up to the window, and slowly opened it and jumped inside. I started waiving to everyone, and told them to hurry up.

Nobody moved, and I couldn't figure out why they weren't coming in. I was getting upset, and it was then I noticed everyone pointing above my head. I turned around and saw Mr. Higgins, the janitor, behind me.

"OK, get back outside, and don't climb through any more windows," Mr. Higgins commented. He led me back outside. I could see everyone laughing at me, but I tried to ignore them. "Thanks a lot you guys," I said. We all then started walking up town.

We walked passed the flower shop, and crossed the alley onto the next block. We stared through the windows of The Ingham County News to see what they were doing. We got bored and went into George's Food Market, and the clerk informed us that she didn't have anything for us to do. Keans 5 & 10 was next door and we decided to go in there.

Mr. Kean was behind the candy counter. I could have stared through the glass all day at the candy. My favorite was Turkish Toffee. They had strawberry, banana, vanilla and chocolate. After about 10 minutes, Mr. Kean felt so bad that he gave us each a piece of candy.

We thanked Mr. Kean and kept walking down the block. We looked in the window of Davis Men's Ware. There were men trying on suits.

We decided to cross Ash Street, and had just passed Dart Bank, when I looked across the street at the courthouse where they were planting flowers.

Whooo! Did that bring back my dream. I quickly told Mandy about my dream, and she laughed. I suggested going across the street to the courthouse watching the men plant flowers for a while.

"I don't know Betsy, I'd rather just keep walking around town," Mandy said. Mandy looked at me with a big grin on her face and said, "I know, let's go to Tony Simone's."

"Can't we wait a little bit, I still want to go across the street to the Courthouse," I said.

Mandy, Chase and Todd all pointed toward Tony Simone's. Mandy said, "Well, we can sit in the booth and practice our belching, and see how loud it gets. You know Tony doesn't care." I didn't really feel like going over to Tony's just then.

Before Mandy, Chase, and Todd took off down the sidewalk, I told them I'd meet them in about 15 minutes. They passed Perkins Hardware and then onto the next block where Ware's Pharmacy was. I looked across the street again toward the courthouse.

CHAPTER 5

Mandy and the others crossed the street to Tony's, and Betsy walked across the street to the courthouse.

Mandy was the first one to the door of Tony's and looked across the street at Betsy. She was walking across the lawn of the courthouse and was watching the men plant flowers.

She still didn't understand why Betsy wanted to go over to the courthouse just to watch them plant flowers.

Mandy, Chase and Todd paid for their cokes and said hi to Tony. They went to the cooler got their cokes, and said down in the booth. Mandy said, "You know Todd your sister can be pretty nutty sometimes."

Todd grinned and agreed, "My sister is a big nut case." They all started laughing and talking about what they were planning for summer vacation.

Mandy suggested after they drank their cokes, that they all go down to the Steele Street School where the summer recreation program was held.

Todd and Chase said that it would be fun, because there was lot to do, and we could see who was there that we all know.

CHAPTER 6

As Betsy crossed the street, she kept thinking of the dream. All the while, that funning feeling was getting to her. As she got to the courthouse, the men were still planting flowers.

Betsy walked up behind the men and said, "Hi." "Hello," one of the young men commented.

"Can I watch you for a while," she asked. "Sure, no problem," one of them said cheerfully.

As he was digging for the flowers, an object went flying off his small shovel. He didn't notice but Betsy couldn't wait to check out what the object was.

It was happening just like in her dream. After about five minutes the men went around the south side of the courthouse. I walked over to the object and picked it up. It was dirty so I wiped it off on my jeans.

It was an old button with the State of Michigan emblem on it. On the back side it had more writing on it.

I almost threw it away, but noticed what looked like initials "JT-HW." It was still dirty, so I decided put it in my pants pocket and when I got home clean it up. I wanted to show it to my mom and dad, to see if they knew what kind of button it was. They probably get mad at me because I picked it up and it was all dirty.

All of a sudden, it started getting dark. I looked up and the moon had started covering the sun up.

I had forgotten that there was supposed to be a small eclipse of the sun that day. It was then I heard a voice behind me. "You found the button!"

I turned to see who was talking to me but there was nobody there. I could have sworn I had heard someone.

CHAPTER 7

Mandy decided to walk to the front of the store and see what Betsy was doing. As she looked out the window, Betsy was picking something up off the ground, and looking around behind her.

Now what is she doing. As Mandy was looking at Betsy, she could see Betsy turning around like someone was talking to her. Mandy shook her head and kept thinking that her cousin was pretty weird.

Betsy felt cold all over, and figured it was because of the eclipse. She decided to go over to Tony's and tell everyone about the eclipse and find out what they were up to.

Betsy walked through the door and saw Mandy, Chase and Todd sitting in the booth. They were drinking cokes and belching.

I paid Tony for my coke, and went to the cooler. After I sat down in the booth, I told them I had found a button and the voice I had heard.

Of course my little brother called me an idiot, and Mandy told me she saw me pick up something, then turn around real fast.

I showed them the button, and of course they all said why did I want to keep it. "I have a feeling that this button is important, and when I get home I'm going to ask Dad about it," Betsy said excitedly.

Mandy told Betsy that they decided to go down to the Steele Street School where the summer recreation project was held and see who was there, and play games before they had to go home.

"Let's go over to the courthouse before we go down to the school," Betsy said. We finished our cokes and said goodbye to Tony and left.

The eclipse was still in progress, and we all knew better then to look directly into the sun. There were other people who were standing on the front lawn holding little cardboard sheets.

I showed them all where I found the button and that's when we all heard, "You found my button."

We all jumped at the same time. This time, when we turned around we saw an image of a young black man in ragged clothing standing in front of the courthouse, but the courthouse looked different.

It was smaller, and we could see behind it. There were hardly any houses, just trees and open land. The young black man looked so out of place. It was like watching someone out of an old movie.

We all looked at each other and decided to start walking down to the Steele Street School. "You found my button," he exclaimed.

Without thinking, Betsy said, "How do I know it's your button?"

The young man said, "There should be some initials on it." "JT-HW, and a union soldier named Henry Worth gave it to me over a hundred years ago, as a sign of our close friendship."

"Yaw, right," my little brother said snidely.

Mandy said, "let's go, we shouldn't be talking to strangers." We all started to walk off, thinking this guy was nuts.

"Please Wait!" he shouted.

I was trying to walk off, when he grabbed my hand. It was weird. I felt dizzy, like I had been yanked out of place. I could, for a moment see an older courthouse, and the young black man. But through the haze, I could see my brother and my cousins holding on my arm pulling me back toward them. Then all of a sudden, I was back with my cousins and brother. They had been yanking on my other arm. That's when I let out a scream.

"Please, you all got to listen to me. I will only be here for a short time," he said anxiously.

Chase had about enough, and tried to push the young man away from us. That's when his hands went through the young black man, and Chase fell flat on his face. We all screamed and ran.

When we got across the street, we looked back and he was gone. The people on the courthouse lawn were staring at us, and then we noticed that the eclipse was almost done.

That's when we all realized he wasn't from our time. We'd all just met our first ghost!

CHAPTER 8

We didn't want to go home quite yet so we started to walk to the Steele Street School about four blocks away.

It took us about ten minutes to get to the school.

As we were walking, we were quiet, trying to figure out what had just happened.

When we got there, a bunch of kids were outside on the field playing volleyball, and we went inside. Todd and Chase decided to play ping pong and Mandy and I decided put a puzzle together.

After about a half an hour, we got bored and decided to start for home.

I asked Mandy and Chase if they wanted to go home first, or come over to my house. They said they didn't want to go home quite yet and would come with Todd and me.

We didn't say another word about what happened at the courthouse. Who'd believe us? No one would believe that I had gone into the past for just a few moments, or that we had even talked to a ghost.

We knew we couldn't tell Mom and Dad yet; and Mandy and Chase couldn't talk to their parents either. They would think we were making up stories. We did that quite often, if we could get away with it.

When we got in the house, mom asked us if we wanted some lemonade and cookies. "Of course," we said. As we drank our lemonade and ate cookies, we tried to figure out what the young man wanted with us.

"I know!" I explained. "It has to do with the Button." I got a rag and some soap and water, took the button out of my pocket and started to clean it. Sure enough, the initials came into view. There were some other scratches on the button, but I couldn't figure out what they meant. The initials that he said would be on the button were clearer after cleaning it.

Why was the button so important to him, and why did my brother fall on his face when he tried to push the young black man?

I knew it had to do with the button, and that was why he had tried to pull me through to his time.

I asked Mandy if she would like to go the library the next day and look up Civil War clothing, and early Mason history, to see what we could find out.

Mandy said she would ask her mom if she could go.

24

CHAPTER 9

Mandy and Chase said goodbye and headed home. After crossing Jefferson Street, they walked past Ball-Dunn Funeral Home.

It always scared them to walk by it. They didn't know how anyone could live upstairs, and have dead bodies in caskets downstairs.

Mandy remembered a time when they were skateboarding down the driveway and saw the truck bringing caskets to the funeral home.

Mandy remembered that she and Betsy walked up to the windows to see if we could see a dead body in the casket.

The only thing they saw was Mr. Dunn staring out the window. That was the last time we decided to look at dead bodies.

Mandy and Chase got home and their mom and dad, "Dan and Jessica," were sitting in the living room.

"So what have you two been up to?" their father asked.

Mandy looked at Chance and said, "We went up town and were just looking in the windows."

Both Mandy and Chase went back to their bedrooms and decided not to say anything until she and Betsy could go to the library, and see what old records they had stored.

Mandy decided to call Betsy and tell her that she and Chase didn't say anything to their parents.

Betsy hung up the phone and let Todd know that Mandy called and hadn't said anything to her parents about what had happened.

Betsy went upstairs and was just about to finish the book she was reading when mom called her down for dinner.

After dinner Betsy helped her mom with the dishes and afterwards sat down and did some reading. It made her tired, and when mom came into the room and said, "time for bed," I was ready.

I fell right to sleep. That night I had another dream, but this time the young black man was in.

He told me he was sorry that he scared all of us kids, and didn't realize that he could pull me through so easily. But he didn't know quite how to tell us that he was from the past.

He went on to tell me that his name was John Taylor, and that he had made friends with a young Union soldier name Henry Worth. Henry had given him the button after the Civil War back in July of 1866, as a sign of their friendship. Henry used a knife to carve their initials on the button.

Henry said that if John ever needed anything to get word to him, and he'd try to help him out. John told me in my dream to come to the courthouse and he'd tell me the rest of the story of what happened to him.

I slept in that next morning and didn't get up until 9:00 am. Mom let me sleep. When I finally got up, I went downstairs for breakfast. Everyone else had eaten, so I settled for toast and orange juice with some scrambled eggs.

Todd was already up and watching TV. I told him about my dream and he screamed, "No way am I going to the courthouse and talking to a ghost."

"Well what are you going to do?" I asked. "I'm going to play at Sam and Eric's house behind the funeral home."

"Ok for you," I responded, "I don't want you to come anyway."

Todd looked at me and stuck his tongue out. I gave him a dirty look and told him, that Mandy and I were going to the library and see if we could find some information on Mason history about the Civil War Era.

I had asked Mom the night before if I could go, but she didn't want me to go alone. I told her that Mandy was coming over and we were going together.

When Mandy got to the house, I pulled her into the den and filled her in on my dream and meeting John in it.

"This is getting too weird," she said, but we both knew we had to find out what happened to John, and how we could help him. We decided afterwards we would go to the courthouse, and see if we could find John so we could talk with him.

CHAPTER 10

Mandy came over about fifteen minutes later, and I told mom we were heading for the library. "See you both later," mom said.

The Mason Library is pretty neat. I love to look at all the different books to see which ones I can read. There's a small room for kids inside the library that we can sit and pick out books that are on the shelves, and read them.

It only took us about five minutes to get to the library. We headed for the librarian and asked where we could look up information about Mason in the 1860's.

She told us that upstairs there was a room that had old newspapers and pictures in it, and copies of the old Ingham County Pioneer Newspaper that was written long ago. She got one of the young aids to show us up stairs, and proceeded to get some of the old newspapers out for us to look over.

We asked for a pad of paper and pencil to write on, and thanked the aid.

It seemed like we looked for hours at different articles before we came upon the one we were looking for. Boy, were we shocked to find out what had happened to John!

The article was about the hanging of a young black man, and three young men who thought they were representing Mason in this cowardly act.

Mandy and I looked at each other and started reading the article. Mandy said softly, "We'll see how it goes, and if it gets to be too much, we'll just take a break and then come back and finish it."

The article was from the "Pioneer History of Ingham County," and was called "Ingham County's One Lynching," by D.B. Harrington.

It took Betsy and Mandy about ten minutes to read the article and by the time they were through, both of them had tears in their eyes.

How could something so horrible happen back then, and nothing be done to get the men responsible for hanging John.

We both had been making notes on a pad of paper about the article and decided to go over what we had read about the hanging.

CHAPTER 11

"Well," Betsy said softly. "Looks like John was lynched on the 23rd of August, 1866, and no two people remember it the same, and was a dark spot on "Mason.""

Mandy said, "Two or three wild, reckless men, who claimed Mason as their home, had a part in the hanging, and the good name of Mason has suffered unjustly.""

As Betsy was talking to Mandy and repeating what she had read, it sounded like the tragedy occurred in Mason, the county seat. It was organized and conducted entirely by persons from adjoining counties and towns, but two or three of Mason's citizens participated in that midnight murder.

D.B. Harrington was editor of the Ingham County News at that time, and the article says he took unusual pains to obtain and publish the facts.

Mandy and Betsy know now that John was a slave in Kentucky, and became a camp follower of a Michigan regiment. He came to Lansing when the regiment returned from the civil war.

John was homeless and sought work. He was hired out to a Delhi farmer, where he remained working for several weeks.

Betsy said, "All John wanted was to earn enough money to buy clothes, attend school that winter, He had arranged with a colored family near Owosso to board with them when the school district commenced."

All John had were the clothes on his back and asked the farmer for some money to purchase a suit.

The farmer refused to pay him for the work he did so the John left. He stayed for a few days with some colored families in Lansing until forced by them to hunt for another job. He visited the farmer two or three times in the hope of receiving his wages, but without success.

John was half starving and had no money, and the clothes were falling off his back. All he wanted was to get his money he earned.

CHAPTER 12

About ten o'clock at night he went to the farmer's house. John was scared that the farmer might put some of his former threats into execution, and as he passed the wood pile, he picked up the axe so that he could defend himself in case of attack.

Apparently John entered the house, and it was dark and went to talk to the farmer. The farmer wasn't there, and John thought it was a trap and started for the front door.

It was dark in the house and he lost his way, and the farmer's daughter saw John and started screaming. The young girl jumped off the lounge and came in contact with the axe, making a slight wound. Her mother and grandmother heard her screams and went out to see what was going on.

They both grabbed John, and he then defended himself. When he turned, he caused a light blow to the side of their heads with the side of the axe.

John finally got out of the house and fled.

Betsy and Mandy looked at each other, and shook their heads. "Why did John go back at night, after the farmer had refused to pay him and threatened him," Betsy stuttered.

Mandy concluded, "After the third time trying to get my money, I would have just taken off and tried to find other work."

"Well let's keep reading," Betsy said.

After John took off, the farmer came back from the fields and the frightened women told him what happened and the news got around to the neighbors.

A posse was organized to capture John and was captured three hours later near Bath and brought back and put in the Mason jail, in charge of the local Sheriff.

CHAPTER 13

By that time the community in the vicinity of the farmers home congregated and threatening vengeance. The reports that were told and retold were exaggerated until it was the belief that the entire family has been murdered.

That was the exact report that reached Mason the next morning. Supposing the reports to be true, the Sheriff felt it warranted to go to the scene and obtain the facts. He went in the company of a local doctor.

After arriving at the place and questioning everyone, the sheriff found out that not a drop of blood was shed from those reported butchered, except from the little girl. No one was seriously injured.

Threats of vengeance and the appearance of strangers in town started worrying local citizens, and a committee was sent to the sheriff asking him to take John to Jackson or some other jail to prevent any lynching in Mason.

The sheriff agreed and assured the committee that there was no danger.

At about 11 o'clock that night several wagon loads of men drove into town. They marched to the jail and there were over a 100 men carrying guns.

A man named Norton from Lansing was their captain and leader. The mob was met at the jail steps by the sheriff and two deputies.

The mob wanted Taylor and the sheriff said they could not have him and was safely locked in a cell and he had keys in his pocket.

The mob then knocked the sheriff down, took the keys from his pocket and broke down the door.

Mandy and Betsy looked at each other and were both afraid to read what was coming next.

"Why did the sheriff tell the mob that he had the keys to the cells," Mandy said.

Betsy stated, "If he hadn't told them he had the keys in his pocket, it would have taken the mob longer to get John out of his cell and maybe he wouldn't have been hung."

"They still had their guns and would have shot John," Mandy said.

"Let's finish reading the article, and get out of here," Betsy said.

The mob took a sledge hammer and broke down the outer door and unlocked the cell. They dragged John out, and put a rope around his neck and he was dragged to the beech tree near the railroad freight house and hung it over a limb.

Apparently Capt. Norton refused to have anything further to do with the hanging, and a man named Cook from Eaton Rapids told John to pray.

John was hung and Cook and two or three others shot him. After that he was taken down Lansing Road and his head cut off and buried him at the side of the road.

Mandy and Betsy looked at each other and hugged each other and cried. "It's horrible what things happened back in the old days," Betsy stated.

"It looks like Mason got the blame, and only two or three were connected with the outrage," Mandy summarized.

Apparently after the hanging, people riding the train through Mason were pointing to the tree that hung John.

CHAPTER 14

It seemed like hours that they had been reading the newspaper article, but it was only ten minutes. Tears were in both of our eyes, because of what happed to John. Mandy and I looked at each other and decided to get out of the library.

We asked the aid is she could make copies of the newspaper articles and put them away. We left the library and started walking home to tell our younger brothers what we found out.

As we were walking up the sidewalk towards Davis Men's Ware, I asked Mandy if she wanted to go over to the courthouse and see if we could find John and talk to him. Mandy still didn't feel comfortable talking to a ghost so I stated, "While I go over to the Courthouse, why don't you go over to Dancer's and check out their clothes. I'll come back in about ten minutes and find you."

"OK," she said. Mandy went into Dancer's, and I walked across the street to the courthouse. I walked over to the small cannon in the front corner of the courthouse and sat on the little cannon.

All of a sudden I heard a voice say, "Little Missy."

I jumped off the cannon and almost fell over. Behind me was John. He said, "please don't be afraid."

I stuttered, "it's going to look pretty weird me talking to you." And don't try to pull me through to your time again. You scared me," I said.

"I'm sorry, little missy," he said.

"Call me Betsy, can anyone see you?" I stated.

"No", he said. "Only you and your friends can see me".

"John," I said, "Mandy and I went to the library this morning, and looked up the old newspaper articles about you." "It was horrible what they did to you, but it was also very dumb of you to go back out to the farm at night and try to get your wages. You had already tried several times, according to the newspaper, the Farmer refused to pay you, and even threatened you," I said.

"I thought it would be different once I left the south, and that people in the north would be friendlier and willing to help," John said sadly.

"You could have avoided all this if you would have just left", I said.

"I know, but I had to try one more time. I got scared, and everything just got out of control, and I ran away," John said.

"What is it you want?" I stated. "And what does it have to do with the old button I found."

CHAPTER 15

As John started talking, he told the story about the old button. The button belonged to Henry Worth a Union soldier. After the Civil War, we came up here with Henry and his regiment to get away from the south.

Neither one of us knew anyone. We had no relatives up here. Henry said he knew some black families and would introduce us to them. So we both came up with the Regiment, and Henry said he'd see if he could get us some work.

When we got to Mason, Henry found out that his dad passed away while he was off fighting the war. His mother had gone off to stay with relatives up north for a bit.

He had no brothers or sisters, and found out that his home had been taken over by others because the taxes hadn't been paid.

He had nowhere to go except to find his mother, and the relatives who lived up north. Henry told John he was sorry that they couldn't come with him, but he knew a few people and he'd try to find them some work if he could.

Henry helped them find work at the lumber mill, and although it would only last a short time, Henry suggested going to the different farmers in the area to work as a field hands.

The day came and Henry said he had to leave to find his mother. Just before he left, he tore a button off his Union jacket and carved both their initials on the button and gave one of the buttons to John.

Henry preceded to carved their initials on other buttons, and kept one on his jacket to remember them by.

He told them both that he'd try to keep in touch and see how they were doing. Henry said that if they ever needed anything, somehow get the buttons to Adam at the lumber mill, who knew Henry and knew where his mother lived up north. Said he'd come help him out.

"Little missy," he said, "my problem is, I'm not John Taylor. My name is Josh Tatum."

"What! That doesn't make any sense at all," I said surprisingly. "The story says you were hanged and then buried and that your head was cut off." "Is this all true." I asked.

"Yes, I was hanged and then dragged out of the jail and hung down by the railroad freight house." "It was horrible, but I haven't had a chance to tell my story till now."

CHAPTER 16

"When you found the Civil War button, at the exact moment of the eclipse, somehow it helped me come back for this short time to get my story straightened out," Josh said.

"But now it's time for me to go. Come back tomorrow if you can, and I'll let you know how you can help me," Josh stated.

With that he was gone. I looked across the street and Mandy had come out of Dancer's and was still sitting on the bench waving to me.

I walked across the street and sat on the bench with her and told her all that happened.

"Boy, this is getting too weird," she said. "I saw you talking to someone but all I could see was a shadow from over here."

"Now what happens?" Mandy asked. I told Mandy we needed to go home and talk about it, and make sure that what we read in the papers was right.

It was getting on to lunch time and Mandy said she needed to get home so off we went.

When we got to my house, my little brother was playing in the back yard and was making faces at us. We told him what happened and what we found out. "So what," he sneared.

"But don't you want to help us solve the mystery," I asked.

"Not now, maybe later", he said.

Mandy said goodbye, and told me she'd call me in the morning. I went into the house and said hi to mom. She asked me how my morning went, and I told her I looked at some old newspaper articles Mason in the last 1800's and made a few copies of the articles.

After eating lunch, I went to the front porch to try and relax. I sat in the lawn chair and read the old newspaper articles again, but I couldn't concentrate. I was confused, was it John or Josh that I talked to, or did I imagine the whole thing? I just sat there trying to read. Next thing I knew I fell asleep and started dreaming.

CHAPTER 17

In my dream, I was back in the old days; I felt like when John or Josh pulled me through. The streets were dirt, and instead of the new courthouse, it was the old courthouse that was built in 1858. It looked just like the pictures in the articles. There were trees and hardly any houses uptown.

It was dark, and outside the jail a crowd was shouting. All I could hear was, "Lets' hang him".

Nobody seemed to notice me as I walked toward the crowd to hear what was going on. I could hear the sheriff, and his men were shouting at the crowd gathering, and the next thing I saw was the crowd knocking them to the ground and taking the sheriff's keys from him.

They stormed the building and a short time later they came out with Josh. The crowd of men had put a noose around his neck and was dragging him across the street to the old Courthouse.

I shouted at Josh, and just for a moment thought he heard me, but as he turned his head toward me several men started kicking and beating him. The crowd stared to put the noose over a tree limb on the north side of the courthouse, but then someone in the crowd said it would be better to hang him down by the depot where people would see his body.

That's when they started dragging him down Maple Street to the Railroad Freight House. I was scared, but I had to keep following the crowd. By the time I got to the old railroad freight house, I saw Josh's body swinging from the tree next to the railroad tracks.

Someone in the crowd told him to keep praying because he was going straight to hell.

I could see tears in Josh's eyes, and he went limp. Shots rang out and Josh was dead.

After a time, they cut his body down, and the one of the men in the crowd cut off his head. That's when I screamed.

CHAPTER 18

Next thing I knew, mom was shaking me awake. Mom said, "Betsy wake up." I opened my eyes and looked at mom and told her I had a bad dream.

"I could hear you from inside the house," she said.

"Sorry Mom, it was probably some of the old stories I was reading about," I said.

"Well, come inside, it's time for dinner." You're dad will be home soon," Mom stated.

I decided that if Dad wasn't too tired, that I'd ask him about the lynching.

We all sat down at the dinner table and mom said the blessing, I always forget which direction the sign of the cross is done, and of course Mom caught me doing it with both hands. All she did was shake her head and looked at me.

I decided it was not the right time to talk with Dad. After dinner I asked him if he had time to talk with me.

He said, "I'm awfully tired, but I can spare a few minutes."

"Dad," I said, "Do you remember anything about a lynching in Mason after the Civil War?" Dad looked at me funny and asked where I heard about that.

How could I tell him that I had met a ghost. "Mandy and I were at the library and thought we'd read some of the old stories about Mason, and went through some of the old newspaper articles."

I told him what I read, and he shook his head. He said he learned it in school, and that it was sad because all the young boy wanted was his money for the work he had done. The Delhi farmer kept refusing to pay the young man the first couple times. The local farmer never thought John would come back a third time. John was scared and the family only had a few scratches.

The story got so out of control, that's when the people in the outlying townships and Lansing thought they would take things into their own hands and lynch him.

Dad then looked at me and said that's how it was back then, but Mason never lived it down.

"Dad," I said, "didn't they ever get the men who did it?" "No," dad said, "every one thought it was best to forget about it."

"Thanks Dad," I said. I went into the den and watched a little TV. It was hard to concentrate. All these thoughts were going through my head. The old papers said it was John Taylor who was lynched. The ghost said he was Josh Tatum.

I didn't understand any of it, but I knew that with Mandy's help, we'd figure it out. I still didn't understand what it had to do with the Civil War button I found.

Little did any of us know, that in the next few days we would all find out.

CHAPTER 19

I got little sleep that night and finally when I did, it was morning.

When I got up, I called Mandy and asked if she would like to go over to Grandma's house to talk with her, and see if she could remember any information on the lynching.

After eating breakfast, Mandy came over and we asked Mom if we could go see Grandma. "Yes" I guess so," Mom said. "Be careful crossing the streets, both of you." We said we would and started off.

We made it up town and circled the court-house on the north side. I looked across the street at the courthouse lawn to see if I could see Josh, but he wasn't there. Mandy and I continued onto Grandma's house. Grandma lived on East Maple Street one block east of the courthouse.

We knocked on the front door and waited for Grandma to answer. We were going to walk in but decided not to scare her. Grandma opened the door, with a big smile on her face, and told us to come in and, she would get some milk and cookies.

I loved going to Grandma's house because she always hid money under the lamps, and when my brother and I were there, we would see how much money we could find.

Grandma asked what we were up to, and we explained to her the project we were working on and the hanging of the young black man back after the Civil War.

Grandma looked at us and said, "why are you girls reading about hangings? You should be reading kids books."

We both looked at Grandma and asked her to please see if she remembered anything. She remembered very little, and said Grandpa would have been the one to talk to, since he worked at the courthouse for years. We asked Grandma if she needed any help with anything and she said no, so Mandy and I left after we gave grandma a hug and kiss, and start up town again.

I got the button out of my pocket, and looked it over again. I had tried to clean it but it was still dirty. It had the marking on the front of the button of the state flag of Michigan. I turned it over and saw the initials.

Mandy and I were at the courthouse by that time, and we sat on the bench in front of Tony Simone's. As I stared at the initials I got a Kleenex out and spit on it to see if I could clean the button any more. As I started to wipe it, I noticed something.

I couldn't get any more of the dirt off so I tried to figure how I could get more of the dirt off the button, then it hit me. My toothbrush, I told Mandy, "Lets go home and see if that works."

We walked home, and Mom asked how Grandma was. We told her ok and hurried up to the bathroom upstairs. We turned on the water in the sink and I got my toothbrush and started scrubbing.

CHAPTER 20

As I scrubbed I noticed something I hadn't noticed before. On the rounded edge of the button at the end of one of the initials was an arrow. Now I was more confused than ever. What did the arrow mean? How could we find out?

We knew it came off Henry Worth's jacket, but how could we find it? It was probably gone after all these years. "I know, Mandy," I said, "let's go back to the library and do more reading through the old records and find out about Henry Worth and what happened to him after he left Mason.

We ran downstairs and were ready to go out the door when Mom caught us. "Where are you two going?" she said. "To the library," we answered.

"No, you're going to eat lunch first, and then you can go." Mandy, call your mom and tell her you're having lunch with us."

"Ok," Mandy said. We ate lunch and then started out for the library.

We got the library and asked the same girl as before about Mason and about the men who had served in the Civil War, and if there was any information on them.

She said there was a section in the library that had a little biography about all the men who had served in the Civil War that told what happened to them afterwards.

We went back upstairs and rummaged through pictures and old newspaper articles. We finally came across one of Union soldiers who was sitting on the old courthouse lawn under the shade trees.

We asked the librarian if she would show us how to use the microfilm machine to enlarge the picture. As she was in the process of showing us, the picture came up on the screen, Mandy and I looked at the pictures of the young men. Underneath the picture were the names of the Union soldiers.

As we were looking through the names, Henry Worth's name was there. Henry was standing at the end of the row and next to him were two young black men.

The caption stated that the names of the young black men were not known, but as soon as we saw the picture we knew which one was Josh. The young man next to Josh looked so much like him, we both knew it had to be John.

It was then that Mandy and I both knew that both John and Josh followed the troops up north to find work. But that still didn't answer the question, if the newspaper said it was John that was hung, why did Josh say it was him?

CHAPTER 21

We both read the article, and it said several young black men followed the troops up north to find work, and that the jacket that Henry Worth wore was donated to the Ingham County Historical Society, along with a letter he had written. Both were in the Courthouse Historical Display.

The librarian made copies of the pictures, and the article. It was getting on toward dinner time, and we were both hungry.

We walked home, and Mom fed us a snack. Afterward we sat on the front porch to talk about what we found out.

The only thing Mandy and I could think of was that John and Josh somehow got switched in Jail; and that the wrong man was pulled out and hanged that night.

But if that was so, what happened to either John or Josh? What did Henry Worth know about the hanging, and what happened afterwards?

"I'm really confused," I said shaking my head. Mandy nodded and then got a funny look on her face, "I know," she sighed, in the courthouse there are all the old Civil War items from the museum."

"Your right, let's go to the courthouse and look around," I said.

We asked Mom if we could go back up town and go to the courthouse. "No, I don't think so," she said. "It's getting late in the day and Mandy, I'm sure your mother will be looking for you."

"Can we go up town tomorrow and go to the courthouse." I asked. Mom said it would be ok.

"Bye Mandy, see you tomorrow," I said. I told Mandy hopefully the Civil War antiques at the court house would give us a clue.

CHAPTER 22

That night I dreamed again about Josh and John. This time they were both together in front of the old courthouse.

I could hear them talking about going to school, and trying to get some work on farms outside Mason.

They both decided to go to different farms to get work, and would try to get together once a week at a friend's house in Owosso.

They wondered how Henry was doing up north, and wanted one day to go see him. They both pulled the buttons out of their pockets and said at least they had this to remember Henry by.

John and Josh made a promise that day that if anything happened to either of them, to make sure one of them got the button to Henry to let him know what went on.

All of a sudden I woke up. I felt like both John and Josh were in the room with me. Mom walked into the room and said it was time to get up.

After I ate breakfast, I talked with Todd, but as always he wasn't interested in the mystery of John and Josh.

Mandy came over about an hour later, and off we went to the courthouse to look at the Civil War museum stuff.

The inside of the courthouse was neat, before you get in the front door, there is an area with bars on both sides of the door where they keep the crooks that are waiting for court.

Usually when nobody was there, we'd lock ourselves in, and pretend we are going to jail. We also try to climb the pillars before anyone could catch us.

As Mandy and I made our way up the walk to the front door, we looked over at the cannon to see if we could see Josh, but we couldn't.

The front doors of the courthouse were big heavy doors, and it took both Mandy and me to open them. We went up the steps and then turned to the right and went down a couple of steps.

CHAPTER 23

The inside of the courthouse was made of stone, and it always seemed so cold. The telephone operator was at her desk. She said hello to us, and asked if she could help us with something.

We told her we wanted to look at the display of the Civil War era stuff. She said to keep walking straight take a turn to the left, and then left again and we'd see the glass cases.

We found the cases, and it was interesting to look at all the old stuff that was there. We finally came across the Civil War jacket with the letter that Henry wrote. The card below the jacket said, *"Owned by Henry Worth."*

We had to get pretty close to the glass to get a good look at the jacket. As we looked, we noticed that there was a button missing from the front of the jacket. On the inside there was a space there two buttons were at one time sewn, but one was missing.

About that time Mr. Hawkins, the janitor, was coming around the corner and came up behind us.

"Hello girls," he said. "How are you, Mr. Hawkins?" we asked politely.

"Good! What are you two doing at the courthouse?"

"We are trying to gather information on the Civil War and the jackets and buttons," Betsy said.

"Well, you are both in luck. I'm just about ready to do some cleaning of this area, and am going to open the glass cases," Mr. Hawkins said.

"Really! I exclaimed. "Is it possible to touch the jacket worn by Henry Worth? I hear they were made of wool, and we'd like to get a closer look at the buttons with the Michigan emblem on them."

"Well, nobody is supposed to touch anything, but as long as I'm here to watch you, I guess it would be ok, just please be careful," he said. We stuck our heads inside the case, and boy did it smell musty. We reached out and touched the jacket. It was heavy, and the material made me itch. We picked up a piece of the jacket and tried to look at the buttons.

We looked at the middle button, as we tilted it over we noticed the initials "HW-JT." Mandy and I looked at each other and smiled. Then, we noticed something else. There were two arrows that went straight up and down.

Now we were really confused, so we looked at the next button above it. Boy, oh boy, the button underneath looked exactly like the button that I had found.

The initials were there along with the arrow pointing to the button beneath it. I had the button in my pocket but didn't want to get it out and have Mr. Hawkins think I took it.

I looked at the other button again, and then noticed a little rip in the jacket lining. About that time Mr. Hawkins looked us and told us to be careful.

"We are, Mr. Hawkins," we both said. I rubbed my finger along the edge of the lining and felt something scratch me. I looked closer and it looked like the edge of a piece of paper folded.

CHAPTER 24

"Mr. Hawkins," whatever happened to the other button?" I asked.

"Well, according to the story, Henry gave a button to the young black man who was hung. After the crowd dragged him from the jail across the street to the courthouse, he lost it on the courthouse lawn and it was never found," he said.

I knew then that I had to wait and not let him know I had the button. Mandy and I both decided it was time to leave. Just as we were backing out of the glass cabinet, I noticed the letter from Henry Worth, with a short note from his family.

Mr. Hawkins said not to touch the letters, but we could read them. As we were reading Henry's letter, it said he asked his family to donate the jacket to the County of Ingham Historical Display in the courthouse.

He stated that there is a missing button, which was the button that was lost on the courthouse lawn when they hung John Taylor. The last part of the letter said that when the missing button was found and put back on the jacket, that a wrong that was done to John Taylor would be revealed.

The letter from the family said it was requested from their father to donate the jacket, but they did not understand why the other button was so important.

The letter went on to say that when the family cleaned the jacket, they found initials and arrows on two of the buttons. They did not know what this meant. They did remember that when they were little, a young black man named John Taylor came to see their father, and gave him the other button.

The family didn't think anything of it at first, but never realized that John was the young man that was hung.

After talking with their father, they found out what happened in Mason and the lynching.

The weird thing was, that the young black man that came and talked to their father, said his name was John.

The family never knew what happened between Henry and John, as soon afterwards, they found out that John died from starvation. After that the family decided it was better not to bother their father about what happened.

Henry had told his family before he passed away, that he had put the initials on the buttons, as a sign of the friendship that developed when he came back to Michigan in the Civil War.

Henry told the family that when they write the letter before they donate his jacket to the County, that on the letter they wrote, that when the other button was found, that the people of Mason would then know what really happened to John Taylor. Their father wouldn't say anything else about it.

Mr. Hawkins said, that everyone who had read the letter over the years from the family, thought that in his later years Henry was confused because it was John who was hung.

Anyone trying to research the history failed to understand how John had died of starvation, and thought maybe Henry was talking about someone else.

I knew we had to get out of there now, so Mandy and I could figure everything out, especially what the piece of paper inside the lining of the jacket said.

We both thanked Mr. Hawkins, and told him we would be back to see him soon, to look at the Civil War stuff again, if we could.

CHAPTER 25

We turned around and started back to the telephone operators desk. As we came up to the stairs that went out the back of the courthouse, I looked out and saw trees and fields and no houses. I looked at Mandy and asked her to look out the doors and what she saw. She said houses and the church. "Why did you ask me," Mandy said. I told Mandy that when I looked out the back door to the courthouse I saw trees and fields and no houses. It was like I was looking in the past. Mandy looked at me and felt my forehead and asked me if I was ok. "Let's go up front and get a coke," I said shaking my head. We started walk and crossed the room to where the old Coke machine was. We put our nickels in, got out two cokes and told the operator we would drink them outside and bring back the bottles.

She said no we had to drink them in here, so we sat on the steps and drank our cokes. After about five minutes we finished our cokes and Mandy looked at me said grabbed me and we then headed toward the back stairs of the courthouse and went out the back door on the east side.

As Mandy and I were going up the stairs, all of a sudden we both felt a cold chill. I started to shiver, and then as we were walking up the stairs, we both started shaking. We both saw a shadow but couldn't make it out. Then all of a sudden the shadow disappeared.

That's when I grabbed Mandy's arm and ran out the back door. "What are you doing," Mandy shouted.

I told her what happened, and she said I saw the same thing and I thought I was going crazy.

We walked around to the front of the Courthouse and sat on the big cannon. We both started talking at the same time.

As we talked, we knew that there were two camp followers whom we had seen in the picture. John and Josh, and they looked so much alike you couldn't tell them apart.

Henry must have given them both buttons. One, from the outside of the jacket, and other from the inside.

I got the button out of my pocket, and both Mandy and I looked at it again. Mandy all of a sudden jumped off the cannon and said, "I've got it."

"What," I asked.

"Take a look at the button again. Remember the two buttons we looked at that were on the jacket," Mandy questioned.

"Wait, I've got it. There was a space on the jacket for one more button," I said.

We looked at each other, smiled and grabbed each other. As we were grabbing each other, we almost fell off the cannon.

We realized then that if you put the three buttons together on the jacket, the two arrows point to the button in the middle.

The family letter said that when the other button was found, the mystery would be solved. When my hand rubbed against the piece of paper that was stuck inside the lining of the jacket, we both knew that there was a message on it, and that the mystery of the hanging, and about John and Josh would be solved.

Now we had to figure out how we could we get our parents to believe any of this. We both knew we had to go home and get both families together, and convince them that we needed to find out what was written on the note inside the jacket.

Mandy and I were so excited. We got off the cannon and started to walk home.

"Little Missy wait," Josh said suddenly.

"Will you quit poppy up like that and scaring us," I shouted.

"Sorry," Josh said, "It's just that I was wondering, what you found out? My time is getting short, and I'll only be here for a little while longer."

Mandy and I went over to the cannon and starting telling Josh what we had found out at the library, and inside the courthouse at the museum display.

We told Josh about the note from the family, and what it said, and about how everyone thought that as Henry got older, he got confused about who died of starvation.

We also told Josh about all the buttons and about the note that was hidden inside the jacket by Henry, but we didn't know what it said.

Josh indicated he was sad to know that John didn't make it, but said it was time to tell us what happened the night the men came to Owosso to arrest John.

CHAPTER 26

After Josh and John came up to Michigan with the regiment, Henry did help them get a little work with the lumber company. That didn't last long, so Henry suggested they try the farmers around the area.

Both of us found families to stay with up in Owosso, and when in Mason would look up Henry.

Henry then went up north to be with his mother, but before he left he gave both of them the buttons. He marked their initials and the arrows, so that one day all the buttons would be back on his jacket, and he would leave a note inside telling people about their friendship.

Josh said he did find a little work, but it was with some farmers north of Owosso. The last time he had seen John was just before he went back to local farmers place to ask for his money again.

After the night John had gone to farmers house and frightened the family, he went back to hide out with the family in Owosso.

The night before the men came to arrest John, both of them had met, and John told Josh what had happened. John was scared and was going to try to stay with some other families in Flint.

John said that would probably be the last time he saw Josh, and he warned Josh to run because they looked so much alike. He was afraid that he would get in trouble because of what John did.

Josh told him not to worry because the family would vouch for him, and his whereabouts at the time of the incident. They both promised that they would see each other soon.

John left that night for Flint, and the family he stayed with gave him what little food they could spare, and told him to keep in touch.

The next day the lawmen came to the house to arrest John. The family told them he was gone and that they didn't know where he was. They didn't believe the family, and started searching some of the houses around the area.

They happened to get to the house that Josh was staying in, and thinking he was John, arrested him. Josh tried to tell them they got the wrong man, but no one believed him. He said he could prove that he was Josh, and not John by the brand on his arm from the plantation he came from. John didn't have a brand because he came from another plantation further north.

Even when he was in the county jail, Josh tried to tell them that he wasn't John. After that, the crowd pulled him from the jail and took him across the street to hang him. That's when he lost the button Henry had given him. The rest is history.

Mandy and I were so upset that we had tears in our eyes. "Please don't cry. The reason I came back was to find out what happened to John, and to let everyone know that they hanged the wrong person," Josh said.

We both promised Josh that we would try to find out what was written on the note inside the jacket. Josh thanked Mandy and me for what we had done. He felt better, he said, knowing that John got away, but was sorry to hear that John died soon afterwards of starvation.

"All we both wanted to get some schooling and find work so we could both take care of ourselves and live a better life up north. I've got to go now," Josh said. With that he was gone.

Mandy and I started off for home, and we decided to tell our little brothers to see if they had some ideas. We felt we needed time to think about everything we had found out.

When we got back to the house, Mom asked if we had fun. We told her we had solved a mystery, but could not tell her anything yet.

CHAPTER 27

Mandy went on home, and I went up to my room to think. I was so tired that the next thing I knew I woke up and it was dinner time.

I knew it was time to tell both mom and dad what was going on, and I knew they would think I was making everything up. So I got all the papers and the button and went into the living room to talk to them.

"Dad," I said. "Do you remember me asking you about the lynching a couple of nights ago." "Yes," he nodded.

I want to tell you and Mom something, and I promise that it's the truth. Both Mandy and I have been working on the mystery of that hanging.

"Why," Dad asked.

"Dad," this is going to sound crazy, but I had a dream last week and it was about finding something in the flower bed at the courthouse."

"When Mandy, Todd and Chase and I all walked up town, I went over to the courthouse and watched some men plant flowers. I found this button," I said, showing it to Dad. He took it in his hands and looked it over.

"This is very old," he said. It looks like it came off a Civil War jacket. I've seen buttons like this when I was young," he said. "But what does this have to do with the hanging?

I then explained to my parents everything that Mandy and I had found out, and told them about the ghost.

They shook their heads, and I could tell they didn't believe a word I said. "If you don't believe me, call Mandy. She is telling her parents right now."

"I'm sorry, honey, it just sounds like another one of your tall tails," Dad said. It was then I started crying. Mom hugged me and said everything would be okay.

I told Dad that if he didn't believe me we could go to the courthouse and look at the jacket, and the buttons on it.

"Dad don't you know someone that works at the courthouse that you could talk to so we could see the jacket and read what the note says that is sewn on the inside," I asked.

"Well," Dad said, "there is Judge Adams. I'll give him a call, and try to explain the story and see if he can meet us at the courthouse." But he's going to think I'm nuts.

CHAPTER 28

Dad got off the phone with Judge Adams, and was shaking his head. "Well," he said, "Judge Adams laughed a lot. He did say nobody has ever understood why Henry Worth said that John Taylor died of starvation when all the accounts said that he was hung."

Dad asked, "Because we've know each other for years, Judge Adams said he'd meet all of us tomorrow morning in front of the display. The judge will call the janitor, Mr. Hawkins, and ask him to open up the glass display. He wants us to bring the button you found."

I jumped up and down and hugged Dad, thanking him for believing me. "Well," he said, "I still have my doubts, but I'll call Dan and Jessica and have them bring Mandy with them tomorrow morning."

"Time for bed," dad said. I went upstairs and once in bed couldn't fall asleep. I kept thinking of everything that was going on, and wondered what was written on the note inside the stitching of the jacket.

In my dreams that night I saw the old courthouse. Both John and Josh were standing in front of it with Civil War soldiers. There was a photographer taking pictures of different groups of men.

Henry Worth went over to John and Josh and was talking to them when the photographer took their pictures of them together.

Henry walked over by the front of the courthouse with John and Josh, and I could see him pulling a couple of the buttons off his jacket. Using his knife, he scratched on the back of the buttons and gave one to each the boys.

CHAPTER 29

I woke, hurried and got dressed and wanted to immediately go to the courthouse, but Mom said I had to eat breakfast first. Dad said he had called the office to say he'd be a couple of hours late.

About a half hour later, Dan, Jessica, and Mandy were at the house. We all decided to we'd walk up town instead of driving to the courthouse.

Mandy came over to me and said, "Both my parents think I'm making this story up and that you and I are doing it for attention."

"I know," I said, "My mom and dad are acting the same way." I told Mandy the only thing we had in our favor was the button, and that dad realized it was old. "The ghost thing, he feels we are making up big time."

We all got to the courthouse and went over to the Civil War display. Judge Adams was there with Mr. Hawkins. Dad introduced Mandy and me, and Judge Adams asked if he could look at the button I had found outside the courthouse.

I pulled it out of my pocket and gave it to him. He looked it over, and then asked Mr. Hawkins to open the glass case so he could look at Henry's jacket and the buttons on it.

Judge Adams bent over the glass case and stuck his head inside. He looked the jacket over, and examined the buttons on the front.

He kept looking at the button I had given him and then at the buttons on the jacket. Finally he placed the button on the jacket in the spot where the missing button had been.

We watched him as he felt along the jacket. His finger hit something. We saw him try to pull on it, but could not get it to move. Judge Adams asked Mr. Hawkins for a small knife to cut the stitching.

After cutting several inches, he pulled a yellowed piece of folded paper out, along with a couple of small old black and white photos.

On the back of the photos was written, It said, "Henry Worth, John Taylor and Josh Tatum, Mason Courthouse, 1866."

We all looked at the pictures, and as Mandy and I looked at the pictures we noticed that Josh had a brand on his arm like he told us. John didn't have a brand.

"Judge Adams," I exclaimed. Josh told me that when they arrested him he told the law about the brand, and explained that John didn't have a brand on his arm. The law thought he was making excuses."

"Well, that still doesn't mean that the wrong boy was hung," the Judge said. "Let me see what the note says and we'll decide then."

Judge Adams opened the old yellow paper and read it. When he was finished, he shook his head. "This letter does explain quite a bit, and I want to read this to all of you." he said.

"The signature on the original letter that was attached to the jacket and this letter matches, and are signed by Henry Worth". Henry goes on to say:

Judge Adams started reading the note.

To Whoever finds this note after my Death:

"By the time you find this note with the pictures, the missing button from my jacket will be found and put on the jacket so that when lined up, the arrows will show where I sewed the note and pictures into the jacket for someone to find someday.

This is to let the authorities know that the wrong young man was arrested and hung that night, and that the lynching by a group of men from around the county on August 23, 1866, resulted in the death of an innocent young man, Josh Tatum. This took place in the county seat of Mason and should never have happened.

This is to let everyone know that the young man who was lynched down by the railroad freight yard was not John Taylor, but his friend Josh Tatum. Here is the proof. These pictures of myself and John and Josh was taken by a local photographer that lives in

Lansing on the Courthouse lawn in 1866 when our regiment got back from the south.

My name is Henry Worth, and I fought in the Civil War. I met these young black men named, John Taylor and Josh Tatum who came back with our unit after the war. Photographers were there on the lawn of the Courthouse taking pictures. If you look at the pictures good enough you'll see the brand on Josh's arm. They both only wanted a better way of life than what they had in the South. All they wanted was to find work and were trying to make money to feed themselves and go to school to get an education. But sad to say John Taylor had just gotten away, and was on his way to Flint to stay with a family when Josh was arrested.

John Taylor always felt haunted by the hanging, and the fact that his friend Josh died in his place. John passed away in 1875 from complications due to starvation.

Those men who thought they were representing Mason hung an innocent you man and got away with murder. Why did we all risk our lives to fight in the Civil War to free the slaves, if these men felt they could do what they pleased and treat these people who moved north the same way the south had treated them. It's a damn shame. I hope that whoever finds this note in the future will let everyone know that this was not the way to do things, Hopefully in the future things will be different.

Henry Worth

CHAPTER 30

After Judge Adams had finished reading the note and looking at the pictures and the buttons, he said he would do some research, but now that everything made sense.

Judge Adams then said, "I'll get a hold of the Ingham County News, and get a photographer down here to the courthouse and, we will make sure the whole story about the lynching, and who was hung, finally comes to light."

"I want to thank Betsy and Mandy for their fine detective work, and for finally solving this mystery," Judge Adams said.

Judge Adams told Dad that he would get a hold of him in a couple of days. After that we all went home and talked about what happened.

Two days later, Mandy and I were back at the courthouse with our families, and the people from the Ingham County News and photographers, having our pictures taken in front of museum display.

That next week the article came out. It caused quite a stir around town. When Mandy and I walked uptown everyone congratulated us and told us what a good job we did.

We still felt sad about what happened to John and Josh, and hoped that Josh's ghost could finally rest.

We decided to go over to the courthouse and see if we could talk to Josh one last time. Mandy and I stopped at Civil War cannons and looked around. As we were looking at the courthouse we saw Josh standing there.

Josh had a sad look on his face. "I'm glad to see both of you today," he said. "I have not much time left here, but wanted you both to know how much I appreciate you letting everyone know what really happened and how wrong it was."

Mandy and I looked at Josh. I told him I wished I could have known both him and John. Josh waived to us, and with a sad smile disappeared.

Mandy and I looked at each other with tears in our eyes. We knew we would never forget this summer.

We decided to take one more walk inside the courthouse and go to the museum display again. The telephone clerk smiled when we walked by and told us what a good job we did in solving the mystery.

We went around to the display and looked at Henry's jacket again. There was another card with our names on it and a copy of the newspaper article on it.

We smiled at each other and decided to walk out the back way. As we turned around and started up the stairs, we both felt cold, and saw the same shadow I had seen before. At the top of the stairs we looked out the back door and saw the pond with Indians camped around it. We were both surprised to see trees and fields and a pond with Indians around it. Mandy and I knew we were looking at the past. We both turned around and looked at each other, then decided to turn around again and go out the back door and everything was back to normal.

Mandy, let out a squeal and we both ran up the rest of the stairs and ran out the back door.

"Didn't you see the shadow and how it looked out the back of the courthouse?" she asked. "Yes," I said. "I saw everything and I don't understand what it means."

Boy, was this summer ever turning out to be the strangest one ever. Why were we seeing the shadow and the past the way the courthouse used to look.

We didn't know then that the next few weeks would be more exciting then the last four. What we were about to find out, no one could have guessed.

ABOUT THE AUTHOR

Rebecca Clinton was born in Mason, Michigan
This is her second book. Her first book is a collection of poetry and prose.
She has been writing for over twenty-five years.
Rebecca graduated from Mason High School
in 1968, and attended Lansing Community College.

Rebecca is a member of the City of Mason Historical Commission
and she is currently working on an autobiography about her father,
Dr. George R. Clinton and Mason General Hospital.

When she was a little girl, her father taught her how to love
the outdoors, and her mother taught her how to
appreciate everything that the good lord has given us.